MAPS *and* MEASUREMENT

Gareth Stevens
Publishing

Please visit our Web site www.garethstevens.com. For a free color catalog of all our high-quality books, call toll free 1-800-542-2595 or fax 1-877-542-2596.

Library of Congress Cataloging-in-Publication Data
Maps and measurement / Ben Hollingum, editor.
        p. cm. — (Understanding maps of our world)
      Includes index.
      ISBN 978-1-4339-3503-9 (library binding) — ISBN 978-1-4339-3504-6 (pbk.)
      ISBN 978-1-4339-3505-3 (6-pack)
    1. Cartometry. 2. Cartography. I. Hollingum, Ben.
  GA23.M367 2010
  912.01'4—dc22

2009037276

Published in 2010 by
Gareth Stevens Publishing
111 East 14th Street, Suite 349
New York, NY 10003

For Gareth Stevens Publishing:
Art Direction: Haley Harasymiw
Editorial Direction: Kerri O'Donnell

For The Brown Reference Group Ltd:
Editorial Director: Lindsey Lowe
Managing Editor: Tim Cooke
Children's Publisher: Anne O'Daly
Design Manager: David Poole
Designer: Simon Morse
Production Director: Alastair Gourlay
Picture Manager: Sophie Mortimer
Picture Researcher: Clare Newman

Picture Credits:
Front Cover: Jupiter Images: Photos.com br; Shutterstock: Mario Savoia

Brown Reference Group: all artwork

DigitalVision: 4m, 4b, 42; Getty Images: Comstock 17; Jupiter Images: Ablestock 5m, 10, 11; Photos.com 20; Stockxpert 5t, 24, 25; NASA: Landsat 40; Shutterstock: Vladislav Gurfinkel 4t; Gary Paul Lewis 7; Alexey Stiop 9; Sebastian Tomus 31; Steven Wright 5b; Yulli 41

Publisher's note to educators and parents: Our editors have carefully reviewed the Web sites that appear on p. 46 to ensure that they are suitable for students. Many Web sites change frequently, however, and we cannot guarantee that a site's future contents will continue to meet our high standards of quality and educational value. Be advised that students should be closely supervised whenever they access the Internet.

Manufactured in the United States of America
1 2 3 4 5 6 7 8 9 12 11 10

CPSIA compliance information: Batch #BRW0102GS: For further information contact Gareth Stevens, New York, New York at 1-800-542-2595.

Contents

The Changing Shape of the World

1400

This map shows the world known to Europeans in the fifteenth century: Europe and parts of Asia and Africa.

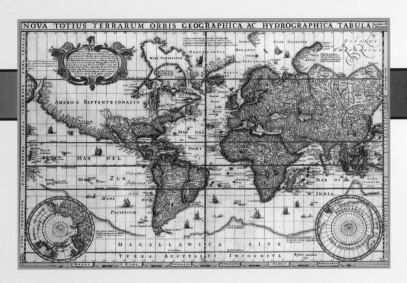

1700

1600

In this seventeenth-century map, only the interior of North America and the southern oceans remain empty.

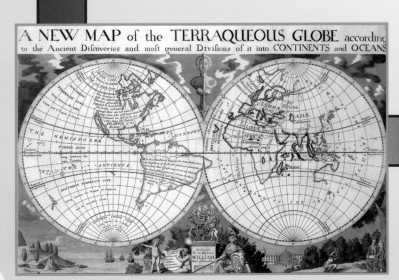

1800

This map reveals more information about Australia, but the northwest coast of North America and most of the Pacific Ocean remain unknown.

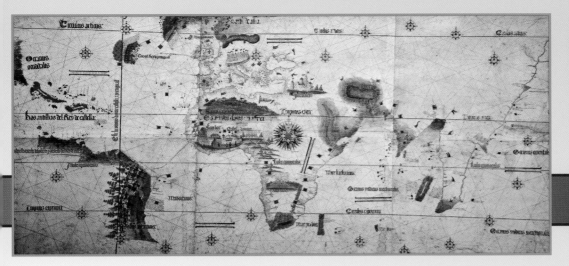

This sixteenth-century map fills in the coasts of Africa and India, the Caribbean islands, and parts of South America.

1500

In this sixteenth-century map, South America is only roughly shaped; the northwest coast of Australia has become part of the legendary "southern continent."

The first photographs of Earth from space were taken only in the 1960s.

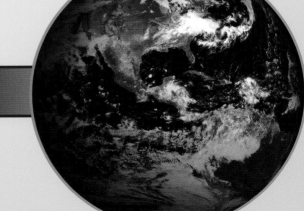

1900

This world map was drawn in 1875, when Europeans were at the height of claiming colonies in other lands.

Introduction

This is a volume from the set Understanding Maps of Our World. This book looks at how maps and mapping help travelers find their way.

UNDERSTANDING MAPS OF OUR WORLD IS AN eight-volume set that describes the history of cartography, discusses its importance in different cultures, and explains how it is done. Cartography is the technique of compiling information for, and then drawing, maps or charts. Each volume in the set examines a particular aspect of mapping and uses numerous artworks and photographs to help the reader understand the sometimes complex themes.

After all, cartography is both a science and an art. It has existed since before words were written down and today uses the most up-to-date computer technology and imaging systems. Advances in mapmaking through history have been closely involved with wider advances in science and technology. Studying maps demands some understanding of math and at the same time an appreciation of visual creativity. Such a subject is bound to get a little complex at times!

About this Book

This book discusses the methods and tools used in practical mapmaking. Religion, philosophy, and exploration have all influenced map production in the past, but it is the influence of science that has led to the most important improvements in the accuracy of maps. Advances in the fields of astronomy, physics, mathematics, and engineering have enabled cartographers to locate points on the earth precisely and create accurate maps. The development of standardized reference systems, such as latitude and longitude, allow us to describe our location on the earth in a manner than anyone can understand, even if they do not speak the same language.

 The development of accurate surveying equipment revolutionized mapping. Theodolites like this one were used to draw highly accurate maps, some of which remained in use for hundreds of years.

Maps Before Science

Before scientific cartography, different peoples built up their own pictures of the Earth and the features on it partly from stories or myths told by their ancestors.

THE IDEAS OF THE EARLIEST PEOPLE WERE A TYPE OF philosophy. They were concerned, in particular, with the place and shape of the Earth and the heavenly bodies such as the sun, moon, and stars. It was only natural that the first maps should develop from these early ideas, and the philosopher's view was the first to be converted into a map. These early maps were not based on observation, nor on measurement.

The first people to base their maps on careful astronomical observation were the Greeks, in about the fourth century B.C. In particular they noted, from the nature of the Earth's shadow on the moon during an eclipse, that the Earth was a globe. It was a different view of the Earth from that of some philosophers, who had suggested that it was like a disk—or even a tree.

The Roman Influence

But civilizations come and go, and as different empires dominated at different times, so ideas about the Earth varied. The maps that came from these ideas also varied. For a very long period in Western civilizations, from the height of the Roman Empire (in A.D. 200) to about 1400, the model of a circular, flat Earth was dominant. It was a return to the idea of the Earth as a disk. In fact, the Roman mapmakers were more interested in mapping the routes within their empire and the layout of cities and country estates than they were in producing accurate maps of the whole Earth. As a result the Greek astronomical observations were mainly forgotten, although some Arab scholars retained the ancient knowledge. The small number of maps of the entire world produced by Romans simplified the shapes of the continents to a simple T-in-O shape.

That is the name given to maps that showed the land shapes of the disk-shaped Earth surrounded by an ocean (the "O" shape) and divided into Europe, Africa, and Asia, the only continents known at the time. The maps had east at the top. The stem of the "T" represented the Mediterranean Sea, while the crossbar at the top was formed from the Nile River in Africa and the Don River, considered to be the boundary between Europe and Asia.

This framework was the basis of world mapmaking in Western civilizations for over a thousand years. During that time people made very few astronomical observations. There were few travel opportunities and not much trading, so there was little need for maps for navigating the seas. The philosophy of the T-in-O shape fitted into Christian views of the world at that time, which placed Jerusalem at the center of the Earth.

Ancient Greek astronomers realized that the Earth was a sphere because its shadow is curved when it is cast on the moon during a lunar eclipse. If the Earth were a flat disk, it would make an oval shadow.

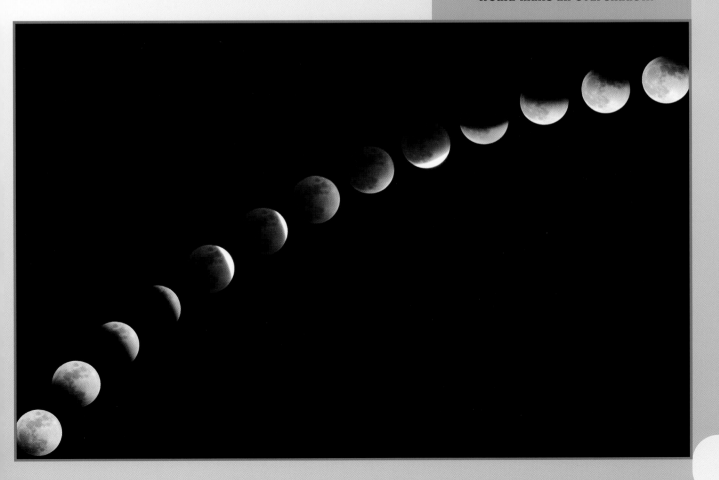

Travelers' Tales

Maps based mainly on the ideas of philosophers were of little use to travelers. They wanted accurate distances and directions, as well as correct descriptions of places.

IT WAS NOT UNTIL THE END OF THE MIDDLE AGES (toward the end of the fourteenth century) that mapmakers in Europe began to change their view of the world. By this time more and more people were traveling longer and longer distances. They needed maps that accurately positioned cities and roads, and revealed the true shape of coastlines.

To produce maps of this kind, mapmakers had to rely on the observations of the travelers themselves. People returning from fighting wars in the Holy Lands during the Crusades or from pilgrimages were able to

This map of the Spanish islands of Mallorca, Menorca, and Cabrera features direction lines. The map includes a compass rose to help plot a course.

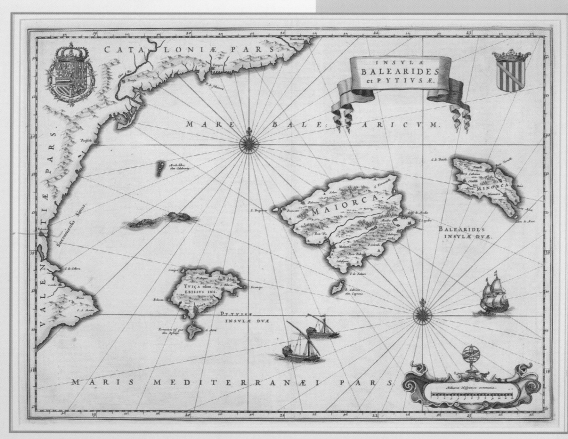

10

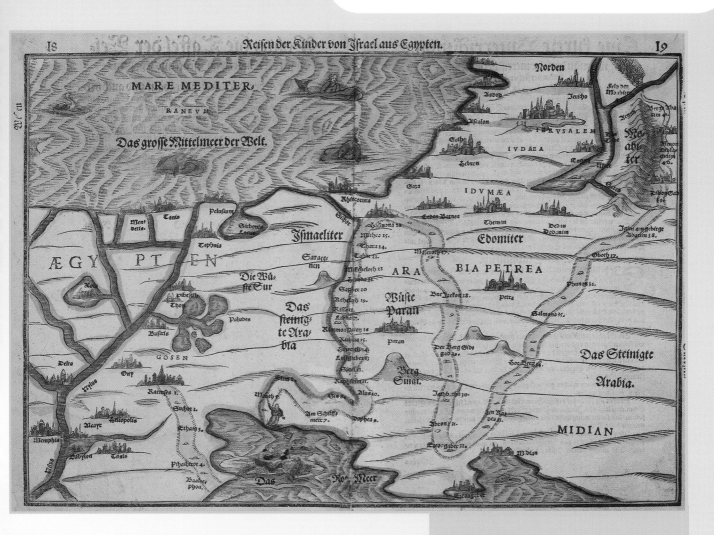

give information on how far apart cities and towns were, their names, and who ruled them. Sailors could provide information about the directions from one port to another.

In the 12th century portolan charts (*portolanos*), accurate coastal navigation maps produced from observations made by sailors, began to appear. These observations were based on readings from magnetic compasses, which came into use during the same time. Direction lines could be charted using compass readings. Navigators surveyed the coastlines of the Mediterranean Sea in great detail and added information about the ports and their rulers. They also included scale bars to help with distance estimates and compass roses to plot a course.

This sixteenth-century map shows the Holy Land and Egypt. The region became widely known in Europe thanks to the Crusades of the eleventh to the thirteenth centuries.

Layer Upon Layer

Topographic maps show the surface features of the Earth. Thematic maps show information specific to an area, such as climate, types of soil, population density, and so on.

THEMATIC MAPS ALWAYS RELY ON TOPOGRAPHIC MAPS as a basis. Both types rely on accurate, but different, kinds of measurement. In order to find out the positions of places, three types of topographic measurement are undertaken on the ground. They are measurements of horizontal distance (distance along the surface of the Earth), vertical distance (differences in height between points), and angles between objects in the landscape.

The technique of making these measurements "in the field" (outdoors) is called surveying or, more precisely, land surveying. The different methods of land surveying are explained on pages 14–23.

Thematic map of environmental problems. Acid rain falls in the industrialized northeast.

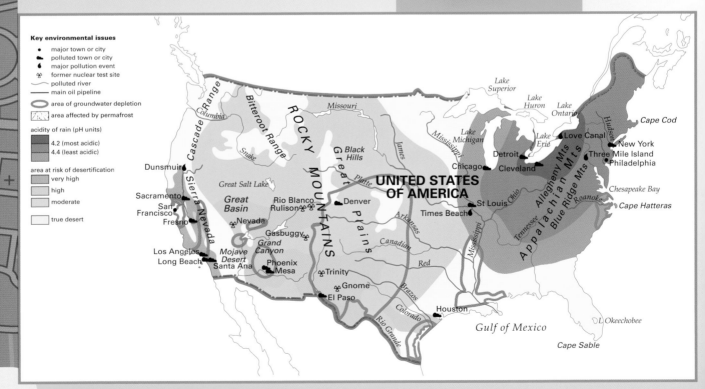

Key environmental issues

- • major town or city
- 🝙 polluted town or city
- 🝙 major pollution event
- ☢ former nuclear test site
- ∼ polluted river
- ─ main oil pipeline
- ⬭ area of groundwater depletion
- ▨ area affected by permafrost

acidity of rain (pH units)
- 4.2 (most acidic)
- 4.4 (least acidic)

area at risk of desertification
- very high
- high
- moderate
- true desert

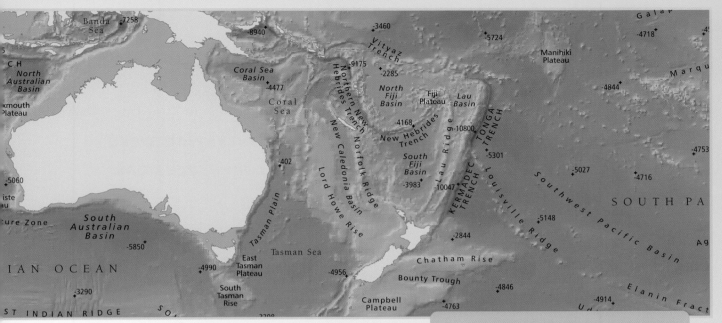

Thematic Information and Base Maps

Measurements of other aspects of an area, such as the weather or population information, are used to create thematic maps. Road maps, tourist maps, geology maps, and air charts are all examples of thematic maps.

A thematic map has a topographic map as a base (to show accurate positions), with a theme mapped on top of it. The topographic map can be simplified so that it includes only those features that are important to the theme. For example, a thematic map showing election results might only show the outline of the states and the major cities. Features such as rivers, mountains, or roads would not be important for this theme, so they would be left out when the map was made. Of course, such a map needs accurate information about the election results.

This is a bathymetric map of the ocean floor. Although it does not map the land, it is still a topographic map, showing features on the Earth's surface.

Surveyors in the field measure three things: angles, distances, and differences in height. With these three measurements a topographic map can be made of any area.

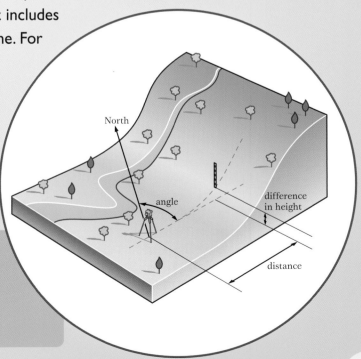

Making Measurements

Observations of the heavens and land surveying were among the very first kinds of scientific measurement. Both use mathematical calculations.

THE GREEK MATHEMATICIAN ERATOSTHENES (SEE BOX, right) calculated the size of the whole Earth. But practical, useful measurements by the earliest surveyors were made over only a small area. Roman land surveyors could accurately measure the dimensions of a country villa and its surrounding gardens. They used surveying instruments to mark right angles (90°) at the corners of properties. Tape measures—or more likely ropes and, later on, chains—were used to measure short distances.

Measurements would later be done over longer distances. John Ogilby (1600–1676) mapped the roads of England by walking along them with a measuring wheel. He pushed his odometer along the road, counting every turn of the wheel. He knew the circumference of the wheel and so could figure out the overall distance.

People eventually made measurements of very large regions of the Earth's surface. Our modern understanding of the accurate shape of the Earth comes from initial surveying work done by

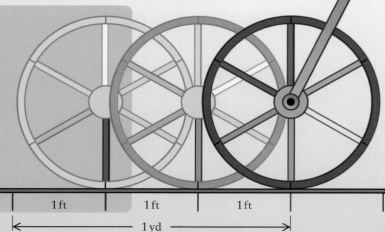

An odometer with a known wheel circumference (the distance around the outside of the wheel rim) is used to measure distances. If the circumference of this wheel is six feet (1.8 m), then as each spoke moves through half a circle, the wheel has traveled one yard (.9 m).

1 ft   1 ft   1 ft

1 yd

French geodesists (land surveyors who measure over very large areas). They went on surveying expeditions in South America and in northern Lapland—part of Finland—during the eighteenth century.

At that time the Earth was still thought to be perfectly spherical. On a sphere the curvature of the surface is the same no matter where you are. The scientists were sent to work out whether the curved surface of the Earth at the equator (in modern-day Peru and Ecuador) had the same curvature as parts of the Earth nearer the North Pole. They found that it did not and that the Earth is therefore

⬇ **Eratosthenes measured the length of the shadow of a pole and therefore its angle to the sun in Alexandria. This angle is the same as the angle at the center of the Earth between Alexandria and Syene.**

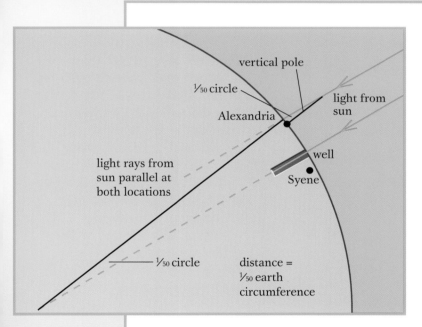

Eratosthenes Measures the World

One of the first experiments that tried to measure the size of the Earth was carried out by Eratosthenes, a famous Greek scientist who lived and worked in Egypt in the third century B.C. He used observations of the sun and measurements of the angles of shadows, along with an estimate of the distance between two places in the Nile Valley. Eratosthenes knew that the sun was directly overhead at the Egyptian town of Syene at noon on Midsummer's Day, June 21—it shone straight down a well in the town, showing that it was directly overhead. At exactly the same time, in the city of Alexandria a lot further to the north, a tall pole cast a shadow.

By observing the shadow, Eratosthenes calculated the angle of the sun in Alexandria. He judged it to be 1/50th of a circle, or 7.2 degrees. Believing the Earth was a sphere, he therefore reckoned that this angle was the same as the angle between Alexandria and Syene at the center of the Earth. So if the distance between the two towns gave 1/50th of a circle at the center of the Earth, then the whole circle, all around the world, must be 50 times the distance between Alexandria and Syene. This turned out to be a very good estimate of the size of the Earth; despite the fact that no one knew accurately the actual distance between the two cities, which was about 500 miles (800 km).

not a true sphere. In fact, it is flattened a bit at the North Pole and the South Pole, and it bulges a bit at the equator. This had been predicted by the most famous scientist of the seventeenth century, Sir Isaac Newton. His theories about gravity and his knowledge of astronomy led him to this brilliant prediction.

Modern Surveying

Today, measurements for mapmaking are made using complex equipment to a high standard of accuracy. Surveying techniques can be used to locate positions on building sites and to plan out the routes of new roads. The accurate measurements of surveyors are even used to work out whether the land itself is changing its position. Surveyors have figured out, for example, that South America is slowly moving away from Africa, making the Atlantic Ocean wider by a few millimeters each year.

Before drawing up a map, you must decide—as all surveyors do—how many points in the area that you are mapping

The Earth is not a true sphere. Its actual shape is spheroid (with the radius at the poles a little shorter than the radius at the equator). The exact shape is even more complicated since the surface is irregular. The distortion is caused by Earth's gravitational attraction and the fact that it is spinning, which causes centrifugal repulsion. This diagram of the earth is called the geoid and is defined as the mean (average) sea level around the globe.

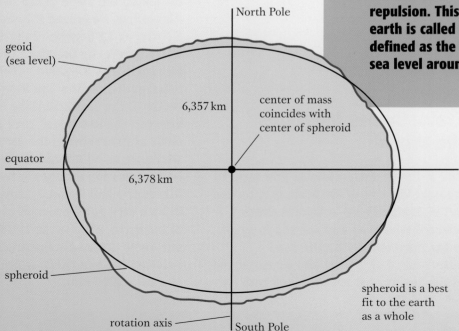

geoid
(sea level)

North Pole

6,357 km

center of mass
coincides with
center of spheroid

equator

6,378 km

spheroid

spheroid is a best
fit to the earth
as a whole

rotation axis

South Pole

you should measure. You could survey the exact location of each house or the exact position of each end of the forest edge and points along that line. (Though you would not want to mark the position of every single tree.) It is possible to do this by visiting all the points with a piece of equipment that can use the Global Positioning System (GPS) to work out exactly where you are (see page 23).

What a Surveyor Measures in the Field

Land surveying relies on a combination of measuring angles (or directions), distances, and differences in height, which together allow us to precisely locate any point that we can see. Using land surveying (unlike GPS), you do not have to actually visit all the points you want positioned. The end result is the same: defining the positions of points on the Earth's surface in relation to each other.

⬆ **A geologist surveys a spectacular canyon landscape in the southern United States. Not only do the measurements allow for accurate measurement they can also detect movements over time that might indicate volcanic action or geological movement in the rocks.**

It is important to start your measurement from a point at which you know exactly where you are. This is called the "zero point" or known point. From this point, or even better, from two known points, it is easy to use trigonometry to work out the position of other points. That is done by measuring angles and distances in the landscape, and building up a series of triangles.

As you can see from the diagrams, that can be done using only angles (measured with an instrument called a theodolite) or only distances (measured with an electronic

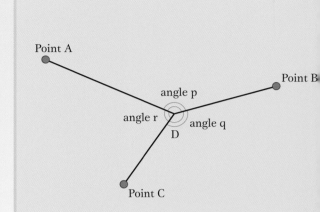

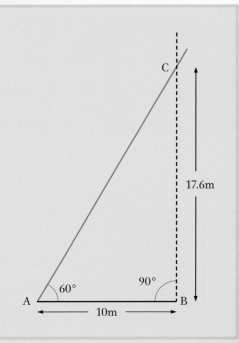

↑ **Resection: If you know the positions of points A, B, and C, you can pinpont position D by measuring the angles p, q, and r.**

↘ **The theory of triangulation is very simple, but it is the basis of all surveying. Imagine you know the width of a room but not the length. If you know the angle at B (90° in an ordinary room) and measure the angle BAC, you can plot the position of the opposite corner of the room, C. You have not measured it, but your scale tells you that BC = 17.6 m.**

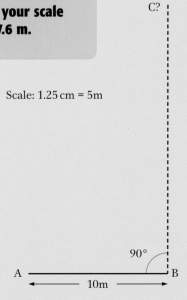

Scale: 1.25 cm = 5m

distance-measuring device). This technique is called triangulation. Once the locations of triangulation points in the landscape have been fixed, you can use techniques such as resection and tacheometry to find the position of any point you choose.

The simplest method of creating a map of a small area is by plane tabling. A plane table is a flat board mounted on a tripod. It is set up at a point on the end of a base line whose length you have already measured. You draw the base line to scale onto a piece of paper on the board. You then look at the directions from the base line to points in the landscape and draw straight lines through them. Move the plane table to the other end of the base line. Line it up with the base line drawn on the paper pointing back toward the first point. Then draw in the directions to the same points you observed from the first point. The precise positions of observed points are located where the lines to the same feature cross.

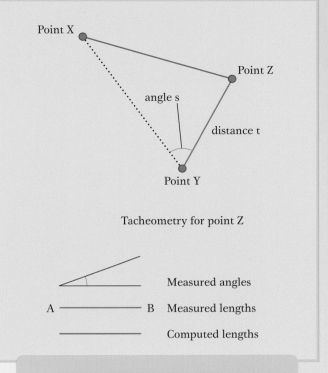

Tacheometry for point Z

Measured angles

A ———————— B   Measured lengths

————————   Computed lengths

⬆ **Tacheometry: By measuring the angle s and the distance from Point Y to Point Z, we can figure out the position of Point Z. The positions of points X and Y must be already known.**

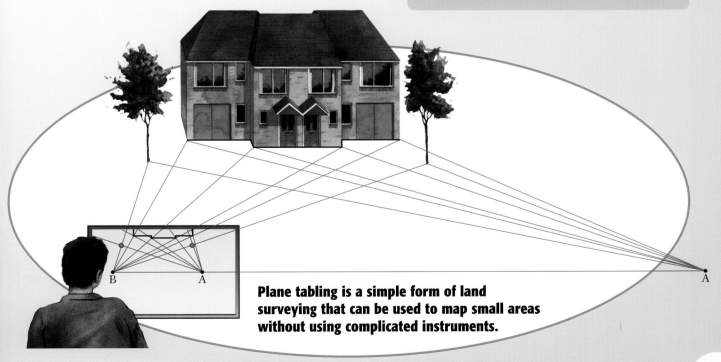

Plane tabling is a simple form of land surveying that can be used to map small areas without using complicated instruments.

Instruments Used for Measuring

Measuring angles in relation to due north was made possible by the invention of the magnetic compass but surveyors needed to measure angles in other directions.

THE NEEDLE ON A COMPASS ALWAYS POINTS IN THE direction of magnetic north. It is possible to read the angle between the direction of any place and the north-pointing needle. This angle, between magnetic north and the direction you are heading, is called a bearing, and it is used a great deal in navigation.

But to measure angles on the ground, we have to consider three positions. Two of them are the points whose difference in position we want to measure, and the third is the point that we are at. So the instrument we use has to be able to see the two distant points while at the same time being accurately set up over the point we are at.

Imagine a protractor placed on the ground. We can read from the protractor the directions to two other points and subtract one reading from the other to figure out the angle in between. This is the basis of a precise scientific instrument called a theodolite. You can set it up at a point, usually on a tripod, and then look at the distant points and read off the angle between them.

➜ **In this 1539 engraving, surveyors use astrolabes to calculate the height of a church steeple.**

Theodolites have powerful telescopes so they can pick out the distant points that are to be observed, and their internal protractor is extremely accurate, usually able to indicate an angle to the correct degrees, minutes, and seconds. All the angles in a triangulation plot can be accurately measured by a theodolite, and from these angles surveyors can figure out the positions of the points of every triangle they choose to measure.

Measuring Distance

Instead of measuring all the angles in a triangulation plot, you can measure all the distances. In the past it used to be very difficult to measure distances over large areas of country, angle measurements being far easier. For this reason most triangulation plots in earlier times used distance measurements as an occasional cross-check.

Today, surveyors use an electronic distance measuring method in the field. An instrument that sends out infrared waves is mounted on a tripod at one end of the line to be measured. The surveyor points the instrument at the far end of the line, where there is a reflector that bounces the infrared waves back to the instrument. The speed of infrared waves is constant. By timing how long the waves take to travel from the instrument to the other end of the line and back again, the surveyor can calculate the distance traveled by the waves. And because they traveled there and back, half that distance is the distance between one end of the line (the instrument) and the other end (the reflector).

Measuring Height

The final measurement that must be made to precisely locate places is their height. Again, we should start from a point whose height we know or start from a zero height

This instrument is called a "total station." It allows the user to measure distances, angles, and differences in height with a single piece of equipment. The onboard processor is also able to perform many of the calculations automatically.

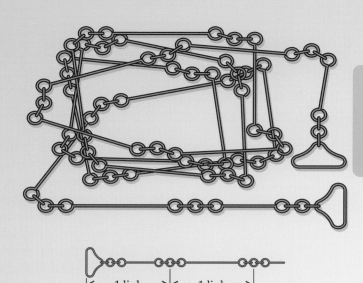

A surveyor's chain made of metal is used to measure short distances. Because it is metal, it retains its shape and length outdoors better than a rope.

|← 1 link →|← 1 link →|

point at sea level. What we basically need to do is to figure out the difference in height using something like a vertical ruler. The diagram shows how an instrument called a level can be used to work out the differences in height between point A and point B.

An alternative is to go back to mathematical methods and work out heights using angles. In addition to having an internal protractor to measure horizonally, a theodolite also has an internal protractor to measure angles vertically. If you know the distance between point A and point B, and also know the vertical angle from A to B, then you can figure out the height difference.

To work out the height at point B the instrument is set up level between point A and point B, and the measuring rods are carefully placed perpendicular to the ground at A and B.
The level is 5 feet higher than point A. The reading on the fore sight rod is 3 feet. So the ground between A and B must have risen 5 ft – 3 ft = 2 ft.

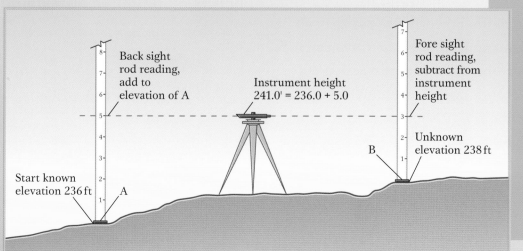

Back sight rod reading, add to elevation of A

Instrument height 241.0' = 236.0 + 5.0

Fore sight rod reading, subtract from instrument height

Unknown elevation 238 ft

B

Start known elevation 236 ft

A

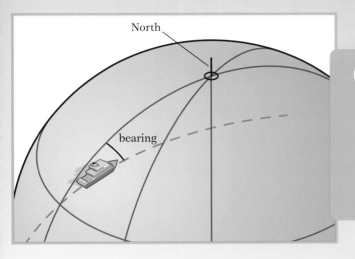

A bearing is the angle between a direction of travel and the direction of north. On a standard flat map a bearing is drawn as a straight line. But over large distances the curvature of the Earth means that following a constant bearing shows as a curved course on the map.

The Total Station and the GPS Receiver

A total station combines the theodolite, the electronic distance measurer, and the level into one instrument. With a total station you can figure out positions using angles, distances, and differences in height, all measured at the same time.

The reason for taking all these measurements of angle, distance, and difference in height is to give us data from which we can then calculate position. Often the position is not actually calculated until the surveyors are back in their office. But today you can get position calculated for you by one instrument in an instant.

That instrument is a GPS receiver. GPS receivers can be put into laptop computers, into cars and trucks, on airliners and ships, and into cell phones. In the next few years you may be able to buy one that you can wear on your wrist like a watch. Although it still has to make measurements of distance (in this case to a number of satellites), the GPS receiver does a lot of the complicated mathematical processing for you, and you end up with a good position— usually in latitude and longitude. Although they are much easier to use than the other instruments described, they are not as accurate as the best land-surveying methods.

Measuring from Photographs

With land-surveying techniques we have to visit the landscape and view every point, but there is a method of measurement that does not require going into the field.

IF WE FLY OVER THE EARTH'S SURFACE AND TAKE A photograph looking straight down, we can record much of the information needed for a topographic map. Features such as rivers, forests, roads, and buildings are visible in our aerial photograph.

There are a few problems with this method. First, we need to be able to identify features from a strange viewpoint—from above looking straight down. It may be difficult to tell the difference between buildings that are quite different in purpose, such as a school and a factory. Second, there are some things that are included on maps that we cannot find on air photographs. We can record street names if we are doing surveying, but they are not in the photograph.

There may also be problems with features that are hidden from the camera. If a forest is overgrown or has its summer leaves fully out, the view of features hidden underneath the trees will be blocked. Buildings and

→ **Although this aerial photograph of a housing development gives an image equivalent to a straight-down map view, it is difficult to interpret. How do you measure the height of the buildings?**

24

A more oblique view of a similar housing development allows us to recognize features more easily. But it is extremely difficult–almost impossible–to take accurate measurements for mapmaking from this image.

roads in the forest will be very difficult to see from an aerial photograph. It is also hard to identify features that are in the shadow of hills or tall buildings. If the photograph is taken from an aircraft very high in the sky, the features on the photo will be small and difficult to pick out.

There are other, more technical difficulties with using aerial photographs. In order for the measurements of features on the photo to be accurate, the camera must be aimed exactly downward. A sudden gust of wind can make the aircraft move around, so that the camera is not pointing down vertically.

Another problem is that tall objects like buildings tend to look as if they are "leaning away" from the middle of the photo, and it is difficult to precisely locate their base.

Photographs suitable for mapping are taken using a good quality camera from an airplane flying steadily across the landscape at a relatively low height. The photographs need to overlap.

If the area we are photographing is hilly, the tops of the hills are closer to the camera (in the aircraft) than the bottoms of the valleys. This means that the scale changes from place to place on the photograph. The higher a feature is, the bigger it will appear. The difference may not seem to be very great, but we are trying to create an accurate map.

The Science of Photogrammetry

There is a way to overcome these problems and distortions, and to take accurate measurements. Scientists have developed special instruments that allow us to look at an air photograph and take measurements from it. Many of these instruments help us identify and interpret features on the photograph by magnifying it. They also let us tilt and move the photograph so that it looks as if it were taken exactly parallel to the ground.

Some of the other problems can be overcome by using a plotting instrument that lets us look at two photographs at the same time. Aerial photographs are taken quickly, one after the other as the aircraft flies along, so that they overlap.

The area of overlap on one photo is viewed in the plotting instrument by one eye, while the same area, but on the next photo, is viewed by the other eye. So we are, in fact, looking at the same area of the Earth's surface from two different positions.

This has the surprising effect of allowing us to see the overlap area in three dimensions. It is called stereo-viewing. If you look at two overlapping photos of the same area in a plotting instrument, the landscape looks three-dimensional, and the mountains and valleys look realistically high and low. In fact, they are so realistic that you can measure the height of the mountains and even create contour maps.

Using a technique called photogrammetry, you can measure the positions of any points on the overlap of two air photographs. You can figure out the distances from one point to another, the bearing of points, and even the height of points above sea level, all without going into the field.

In fact, some field work is still required. In order to find our origin point and set up our references for the measurements from the photographs, we need to know the accurate positions of a few points on the overlap area. Surveying finds the positions of perhaps five or six points, and then the mapping of the whole landscape using photogrammetry is done in the office.

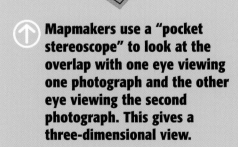

Mapmakers use a "pocket stereoscope" to look at the overlap with one eye viewing one photograph and the other eye viewing the second photograph. This gives a three-dimensional view.

Latitude and Longitude

In addition to accurate measurements of the topography of places, the mapmaker needs to know where places are in relation to each other on the surface of the globe.

THE WAY IN WHICH POINTS CAN BE DEFINED ACROSS the whole world is by using a pattern of lines on a globe. This set of lines is called a graticule, and it defines any position on a sphere (the Earth is nearly a perfect sphere).

The main fixed points on the Earth's surface that help define this pattern of lines are the geographic North Pole and the geographic South Pole. They are fixed because the Earth rotates around the straight line that goes between them through the center of the Earth.

Longitude

The graticule consists of two different types of line. The lines running from the North Pole to the South Pole are lines of longitude, sometimes called meridians, and they are used to show

The graticule (left) is like a net holding a ball. It is obvious why the lines of latitude (below) are sometimes called parallels. If we cut the world in half (below right), we can see how it can be divided into segments. These segments are marked out by the lines of longitude.

Equator

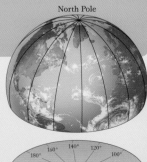

North Pole

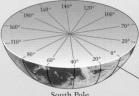

South Pole

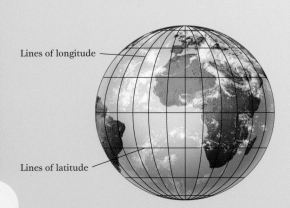

Lines of longitude

Lines of latitude

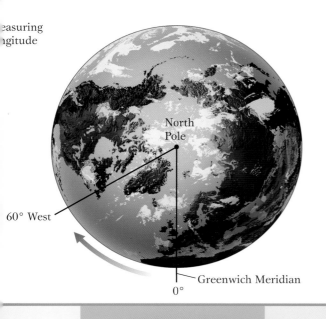

Measuring longitude

North Pole

60° West

0° — Greenwich Meridian

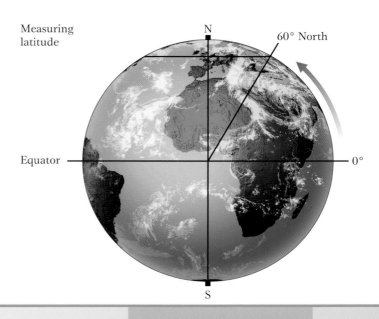

Measuring latitude

N

60° North

Equator — 0°

S

↑ **The "zero position" for longitude is the Greenwich Meridian.**

↑ **The "zero position" for lines of latitude is the equator.**

how far east or west you are. Because each meridian runs from the North Pole to the South Pole, they are all the same length. The meridians are spread out evenly around the circumference of the Earth and can therefore be measured in degrees of a circle. So there is one line of 0 degrees longitude.

If you start on that line and travel west around the Earth, you reach 180 degrees west halfway around. You have traveled completely within the western hemisphere. If you travel east, in the eastern hemisphere, you reach the same halfway point at 180 degrees east. Longitude is stated in degrees east or west, for example, "59 degrees East."

Latitude

The second set of lines runs across the lines of longitude at right angles. They are the lines of latitude, sometimes called parallels. The latitude measures how far north or south a point is. The northern hemisphere consists of all the Earth between the equator and the North Pole, while the southern hemisphere is all the Earth between the equator and the South Pole. The equator is defined as the line of 0 degrees latitude, and it is a fixed line. It encircles the Earth at its longest circumference and is always exactly halfway between the North and South Poles. Ninety degrees north is the position of the North Pole, and there the latitude is not a line but only a single point.

Specifying Position

We can specify our position in terms of degrees—and minutes and seconds if we are being precise—of longitude (east or west) and of latitude (north or south).

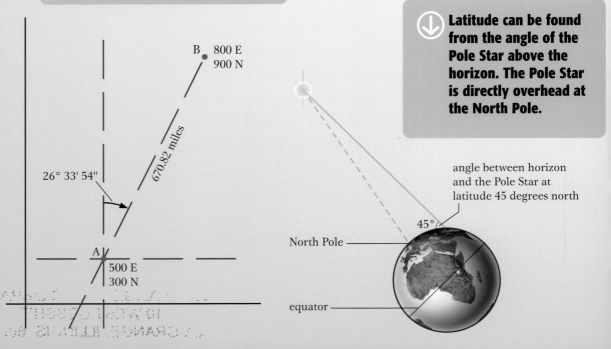

Determining position by angle and distance; we can figure out the grid coordinates of point B from the coordinates of point A, the bearing of the line from A to B, and the distance between them.

B 800 E
   900 N

670.82 miles

26° 33' 54"

A
500 E
300 N

Latitude can be found from the angle of the Pole Star above the horizon. The Pole Star is directly overhead at the North Pole.

angle between horizon and the Pole Star at latitude 45 degrees north

45°

North Pole

equator

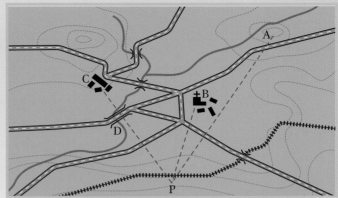

A rough form of resection is to just line up your map with landmarks that you can see. So position P is found by observing A, B, C, and D.

GPS also works using this coordinate system, making it the preferred method of recording your position.

This method of position fixing is complicated, however, by the need to compensate for the spherical nature of the earth, which makes it difficult to calculate accurately the distances between positions given in latitude and longitude. At the equator, for example, the physical distance between two meridians is far greater than it would be nearer the poles.

The basic requirement in positioning is to recognize where known points are located. Measuring bearing and distance from such points helps calculate the positions of other points. Alternatively, if a number of known points are visible, resection can be used (see page 18). As with triangulation, we can do resection by measuring angles or distances, or both.

A simple form of resection by angle is to orientate a map by lining it up with features such as distant hilltops, or buildings and rivers. This gives us a rough estimate of our position.

Working out our position in height is a little more difficult. We rely on a known "zero point," in this case sea level, where the elevation is zero. If we can see down to the seashore and observe a vertical angle to it, and we know how far away it is, it is possible to figure out our own height.

Height above sea level is calculated from the angle down to the sea and the distance.

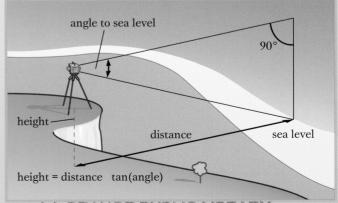

angle to sea level

90°

height

distance

sea level

height = distance tan(angle)

Using Coordinates

The most important information shown on a map is the precise location of places. To show positions correctly the mapmaker employs a coordinate system.

THE COORDINATE SYSTEM THAT COVERS THE WHOLE world is the graticule of longitude and latitude lines discussed on pages 28–31. It is the most common grid system used for navigation. By reading the coordinates, mapmakers can all agree on a precise location for any place on Earth. When plotting and reading latitude and longitude, latitude is given first followed by longitude. The location of Mount Everest in the Himalayas, for example, is 27°N 86°E. These are the mountain's coordinates. No matter what differences there may be in map styles and kinds of information provided, they will all agree on the latitude and longitude coordinates.

Grid Coordinates

Latitude and longitude are not the only coordinates used on maps. The diagram to the right shows how you can use graph paper to

The grid on this map of Crete helps the map reader find archeological sites marked by the purple numbers. A site list provided would give number and grid reference. For example, "52 Petsofas: F2." It could also provide information about the site: "2nd-century B.C. sculptures," for example.

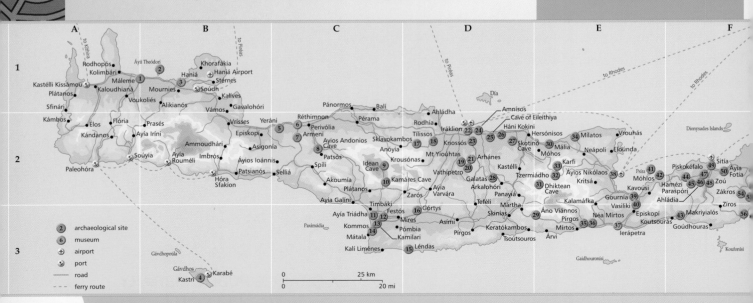

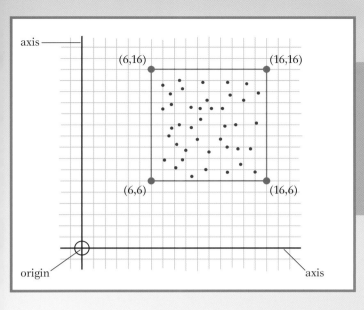

axis

(6,16)   (16,16)

(6,6)   (16,6)

origin   axis

Using graph paper to create a coordinate system. Count the lines from the origin, or "zero point," upward 6 and across 6 to find the coordinates of the bottom lefthand corner of the square 6, 6. All of the points inside the square have two-figure coordinates between 6, 6 and 16, 16.

create a coordinate system. Grid systems like this normally take the form of letters along the horizontal grid line and numbers for the vertical grid. On the Crete map to the left, Hania Airport is located on the map in the grid known as B1 (2 along and 1 down).

As well as showing the positions of places and features, maps can also plot other information called attributes. For example, the names of the archeological sites on the Crete map are attributes. A number in a blue circle indicates the presence of a museum. That might not be all there is at that location, but it is the attribute shown by the map.

Features on the Earth's surface have position and attributes. The geology and population of the town are attributes.

The height and position of a mountain can be read on a map without a label. Location is not an attribute.

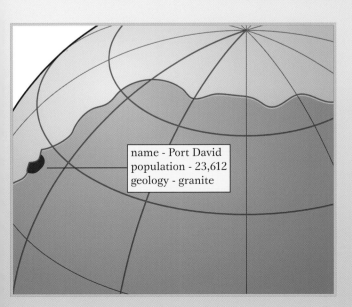

name - Port David
population - 23,612
geology - granite

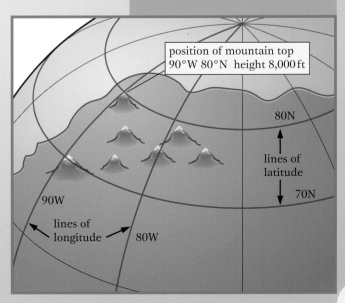

position of mountain top
90°W 80°N height 8,000 ft

80N

lines of latitude

70N

90W

lines of longitude   80W

Scale

Mapmakers have to fit information about distance, size, and position into a small, flat area in such a way as to reflect the true scale of distances and sizes on Earth.

THIS MEANS THAT THE MAJOR CHARACTERISTIC OF A map is the fact that it is a scaled representation of the real world. If mapmakers were to show the Earth at a scale at which everything is the same size as it is in reality, you would have a map with the same dimensions as the Earth itself—you could not fold it up and put it in your pocket!

Instead, a lot of information about the Earth can be squeezed onto a map on a single sheet of paper or a computer screen by scaling it down. A map of North America on one page, for example, might show the Colorado River, which is really 1,422 miles (2,288 km) in length, using a blue line symbol only 2 inches (5 cm) long. (See map below.)

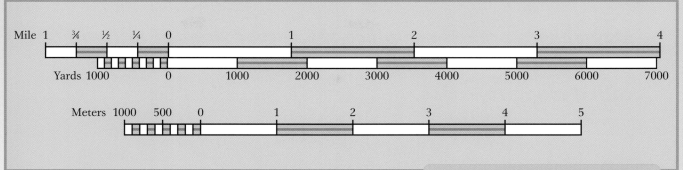

Describing the Scale

The distance on the map is related to the distance in the real world by the scale of the map. In words, the scale is: "2 inches to 1,422 miles." This is simplified using elementary math. If 2 inches represents 1,422 miles, then one-half of the map distance—1 inch—represents 711 miles (1,422 divided by 2). The scale is "1 inch to 711 miles."

We can also show the scale in numerical terms using a representative fraction: "1 inch/711 miles" or "1 inch: 711 miles." The 711 miles can be converted to 3,754,080 feet, which also equals 45,048,960 inches. The true representative fraction, therefore, is 1:45,048,960. This fraction, or ratio, has no units—inches or miles—at all. This unit-free representative fraction is valid whatever measuring system we use to get information from the map.

It is also possible to show the scale graphically using a scale bar, which has markers dividing it into real-world units. If you want to work out a distance on a map, you can measure it and then compare that measurement with the scale bar.

The two bars above show types of graphical map scale that can be used to figure out distances measured on the map. The top scale bar is in Imperial measurement, miles and yards; the bottom bar is metric, in meters and kilometers.

The mainland U.S. states and their capital cities, along with major rivers and lakes. At the bottom is the representative fraction 1:45,048,960 and the scale bar given in both metric (km) and Imperial (miles) units. On this scale the Colorado River is about 2 inches long.

Map Projections

Mapmakers are able to place the curved lines of latitude and longitude onto a flat surface by using a method called map projection.

THERE ARE A LARGE NUMBER OF DIFFERENT MAP projections, each of which is a method of taking a position or area on the curved surface of the Earth and plotting it, to scale, on a flat piece of paper. Many of these methods can involve complicated mathematical formulas that take the latitude and longitude, defining the position accurately on the Earth's surface, and transform them into coordinates that can be plotted in the same way that a graph is plotted.

It is possible to think of some map projections in a nonmathematical way. If the lines of latitude and longitude (graticules) drawn on the globe are projected onto a flat piece of paper as shadows created from a light source, we can visualize these projections as a pattern.

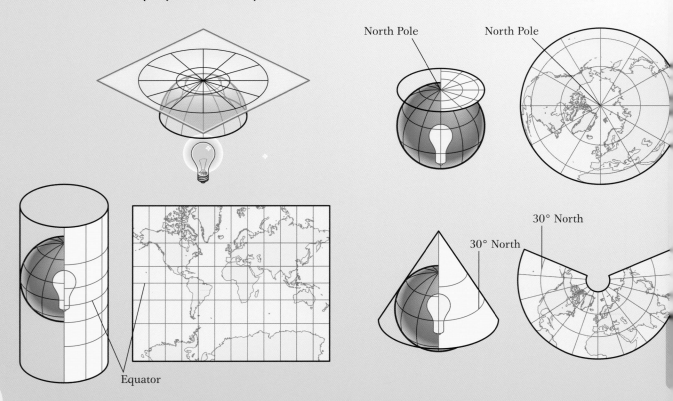

North Pole   North Pole

Equator

30° North   30° North

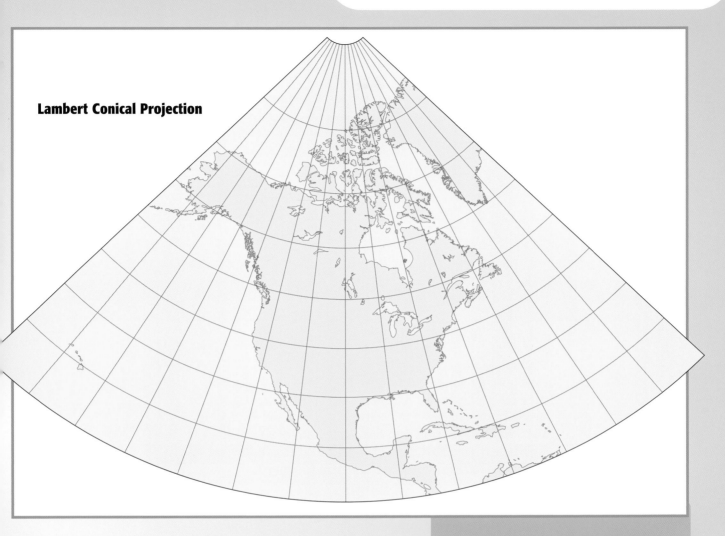

Lambert Conical Projection

The first diagram to the left shows a piece of paper touching the globe at the North Pole, with a light in the center of the globe projecting the shadows of the graticule onto it. If we placed the light on the far side of the globe to the paper or took it really far away, the pattern of lines would be different.

The layout of the shadow lines (the projection) would be changed again if the piece of paper was rolled up around the globe like a cylinder and then unrolled to a flat surface.

In a big country like the United States more than one projection may be used at a local level. For states long east to west the Lambert conical projection shows area well. For states long north to south the Mercator is better.

Projections can be visualized as the pattern of lines of latitude and longitude cast onto a piece of paper as shadows from an imaginary light source. The diagrams to the left show various possibilities in which either the light or the piece of paper is positioned differently to produce different projections.

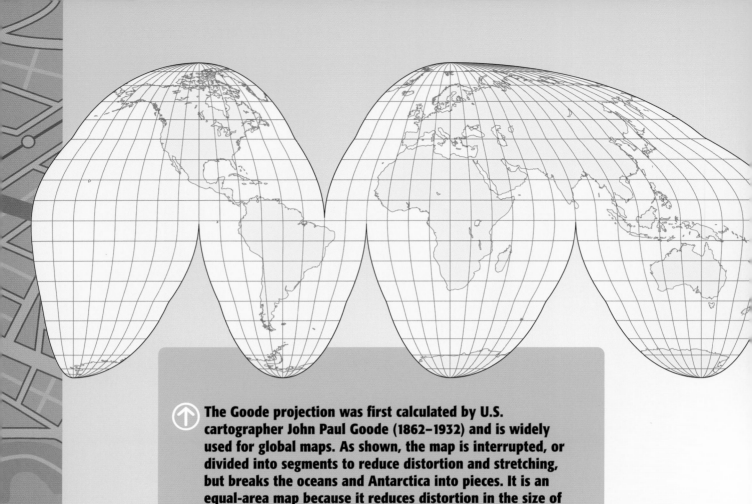

↑ **The Goode projection was first calculated by U.S. cartographer John Paul Goode (1862–1932) and is widely used for global maps. As shown, the map is interrupted, or divided into segments to reduce distortion and stretching, but breaks the oceans and Antarctica into pieces. It is an equal-area map because it reduces distortion in the size of landforms, although Antarctica is still too large.**

(Mercator's projection is cylindrical.) If it was rolled into a cone that sat like a hat on the globe and had shadows projected onto it, the result is another, different pattern.

Each of these shadow patterns is a projection, and they each have different graticules. The shape of the features on the Earth's surface, like the outline of the continents, is different on each one. The positions of places on the Earth have been transformed by different mathematical calculations for each projection.

Lots of Projections—None of Them Perfect

Why do we need many different projections? The main reason is that each projection has advantages and disadvantages in showing the properties of the real world.

The only "true" representation of the Earth to scale is a globe, because that is the only way that we can show the correct

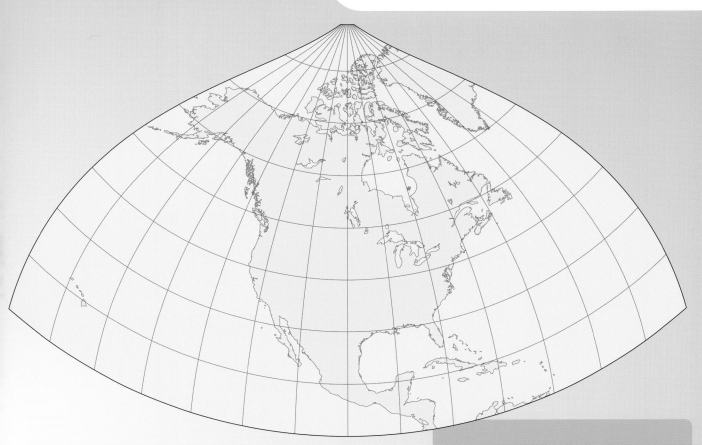

relationship between points on the Earth's surface. From a globe we can figure out the true distance between places, the true bearing (direction) from one place to another, and the true size of an area of land. With a map projection onto a flat surface it is impossible to ensure that all three of these properties are maintained. Map projections always have to show at least one of them incorrectly.

The Mercator projection—a projection is named after the person who first calculated it—gives us true bearing, but does not give us true area (South America looks the same size as Greenland but is in fact nine times bigger).

Because there are many different projections, cartographers have to decide which one is best for showing a particular theme. A map showing the vegetation of the world would be best on a true-area projection, but a map showing distances between world cities should be on a true-distance projection.

⬆ **The Bonne projection was first calculated by Rigober Bonne in the mid-1700s and is ideal for mapping mid-latitude countries such as the United States. All parallel lines are divided equally, and the connecting curves make the meridians. Scale is true along the central meridian (number 8 of the 15 lines of longitude shown above) and along all parallels.**

Glossary

Words in *italics* have their own entries in the glossary.

acid rain – rain or other form of precipitation that contains high levels of acid as a result of absorbing waste gases in the atmosphere. It causes environmental damage to vegetation, crops, and buildings.

aerial photograph (or air photograph) – a photograph looking straight down at Earth, taken from an airplane

altitude – height or vertical distance above mean sea level; or the degrees of elevation of a star, the sun, or the moon above the horizon

archaeology – the science of interpreting the past by examining remains, usually dug up from under the ground

astrolabe – an early disk-shaped instrument used for measuring the altitude of stars above the horizon

astronomy – the scientific study of celestial bodies (planets and stars) and of the universe as a whole. People who do this are called astronomers.

attribute – a particular characteristic of an object or feature on a map, such as the pollution in a lake or the name of a building

base map – a map that shows basic data, fundamental cartographic information such as political boundaries and topography (see also Topographic map)

base line – to perform a *triangulation*, or when *plane tabling*, a base line must be measured on the ground between two points and drawn to scale, from which angles can be measured, directions plotted, and distances calculated

bathymetric maps or charts – those that show the depths of oceans, seas, and lakes

bearing – the direction someone is heading measured as an angle away from north; due north has a bearing of 0 degrees, while due west has a bearing of 270 degrees. Bearing is also sometimes used to describe angular position or direction in relation to any two known points.

An aerial photograph of the crowds gathered for the inauguration of President Barack Obama in January 2009. This picture was taken from an aircraft flying below cloud-level for a better view.

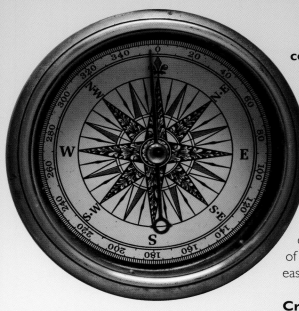

The compass was an essential tool for navigators until the late-twentieth century, and is still widely used.

cartographer – someone who collects information and produces maps; the task of making maps is called cartography

centrifugal repulsion – movement away from a center of rotation as the result of force exerted by a body (such as the earth) constrained to move in a curved path

circumference – the external boundary or surface of a solid object; the circumference of the earth is usually taken as the distance around the equator

chain – a set of linked metal rods accurately made to be a certain length; the land surveyor can use a chain to measure short distances

compass – an instrument showing the direction of *magnetic north* using a magnetic needle; *bearing* can be calculated by using a compass

compass rose – a diagram showing 360 degrees of *bearings*, placed on old maps to help navigators

contour – an imaginary line connecting places in the landscape that are at equal height above (or below) *sea level*. The distance of contour lines from each other on a map shows how steeply or gradually land rises.

coordinates – the pair of values that define a position on a graph or on a map with a coordinate system (such as *latitude* and *longitude*). On a map the coordinates "55°N 45°E" indicate a position of 55 degrees north of *latitude*, 45 degrees east of *longitude*.

Crusades – in the Middle Ages (eleventh to thirteenth centuries) military expeditions of Christian armies from Europe against the Moslems of the Middle East

eclipse – the total or partial obscuring of one celestial body by another. In a solar eclipse the moon passes in front of the sun, preventing light from reaching Earth. When Earth comes between the sun and the moon (lunar eclipse), a shadow of Earth is cast onto the moon.

electronic distance measuring – the use of an electronic device to send out a signal along a line to be measured, timing its path from one end of the line to a reflector at the other end, and back again; then figuring out the line distance

elevation – angular or vertical distance from the Earth's horizon or from sea level to a higher object or point

equal-area map – a map that shows any part of Earth's surface in the correct proportion when compared with any other part. You would think that all maps do this, but because the world is round, such maps do not show the distances between places, or the directions, accurately; so equal-area maps are not always the best choice.

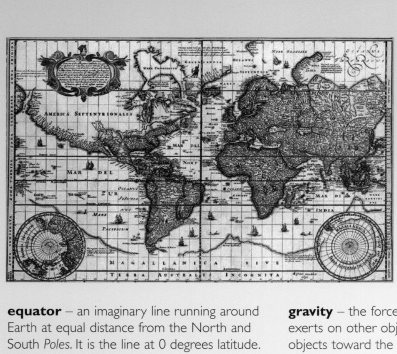

The Mercator projection was an important advance in the science of cartography. It allowed the curved surface of Earth to be represented as a two-dimensional image without distorting the lines of latitude and longitude. This made it ideal for navigators.

equator – an imaginary line running around Earth at equal distance from the North and South *Poles*. It is the line at 0 degrees latitude.

geodesists – scientists concerned with determining the exact position of points on Earth's surface, and the shape and size of Earth

geoid – the surface around Earth, coinciding with mean, or average, *sea level*

geologist – somebody who studies of the origin, history, and structure of Earth

geometry – math concerned with the relationship between points, lines, and surfaces

Global Positioning System (GPS) – a system of 24 man-made satellites orbiting Earth and sending out highly accurate radio signals indicating where they are; a GPS receiver held by someone on the earth can interpret the signals and calculate the receiver's position on Earth

globe –Earth; or a map of Earth produced on a sphere

graticule – the mesh of lines of *latitude* and *longitude* that is presented on maps as covering Earth; the graticule is one example of a *grid system*

gravity – the force that a celestial body exerts on other objects; the force that pulls objects toward the center of Earth and gives them weight

grid system – a *reference system* that uses a mesh of horizontal and vertical lines over the face of a map to pinpoint the position of places. The mesh of lines often helps show distance of locations east and north from a set position. The *zero point* can be any convenient location and is often the bottom-left corner of the map.

hemisphere – one-half of the *globe*. Earth is divided into northern and southern hemi-spheres by the *equator* and into western and eastern hemispheres by the *Prime Meridian*.

hydrographic surveying – the measurement of depths at sea by specialized survey ships to collect information for creating maps used by sailors

infrared – a part of the spectrum close to red, but detected by the senses as heat, rather than light; infrared radiation is not visible to the eye but can be recorded by some sensors

latitude – a line that joins places of equal angular distance from the center of Earth in a north-south direction. The *equator* is at 0 degrees latitude, the *poles* at 90 degrees latitude north and south

level – a *surveying* instrument used to figure out the difference in height between points close together on Earth's surface

lodestone – a hard, black stone (a type of magnetite) that attracts iron and steel as a magnet does; used as an early navigational aid

longitude – a line connecting places of equal angular distance from the center of Earth, measured in degrees east or west of the *Prime Meridian*, which is at 0 degrees longitude

magnetic north – the northerly direction in Earth's magnetic field, indicated by the direction in which a *compass* needle points, at an angle from the true (geographic) north

map projection – a method of representing the curved surface of Earth on a flat piece of paper or on a computer screen. Different projections use varying kinds of *grid systems* to plot locations.

meridians – lines of *longitude*

Mercator projection – a *map projection* named after its deviser Gerardus Mercator (1512–1594), which is commonly used in making nautical charts; *bearings* are shown as straight lines on this projection

oblique view – a view of the Earth's surface from above, not looking straight down but at an angle to the surface

odometer – a device for recording distance on land, particularly along roads. A wheel with a known circumference rotates across the ground, and distance is calculated by counting the number of revolutions between locations and multiplying by the circumference.

orientate – to position a map or *surveying* instrument, or a person, with reference to known features or to the points of the *compass*.

The word comes from the Latin *oriens*, which means "rising" and refers to the sun, which rises in the east. So "the Orient" came to mean countries east of the Mediterranean.

origin – the place in a coordinate system where the coordinate pair reads (0, 0)

parallels – lines of *latitude*

philosophy – a set of beliefs about the world; a personal outlook or viewpoint

photogrammetry – the science of extracting accurate measurements from photographs of the world

plane tabling – a simple *surveying* technique that allows a reasonably accurate map to be created in the field over small, compact, open areas, using a drawing board

plotting instrument – an instrument used in *photogrammetry* that adjusts distortions in photographs to produce accurate measurements for mapmaking purposes

poles – the points at either end of Earth's axis of rotation where it meets Earth's surface; the Geographic North and South Poles

Pole Star – sometime called Polaris, it is the closest star in the northern *hemisphere* night sky to the northern celestial pole; facing it, therefore, indicates that you are facing north

portolan charts – navigational charts used by European sailors from about 1300 to 1600

Prime Meridian – the line of *longitude* at 0 degrees; by international agreement it is the line that passes through Greenwich, London, England

ratio – in math, the expression of one number divided by another; concerning maps, the important ratio is the expression of one unit of distance on the map divided by the actual distance it represents in the real world. This is the *scale* of the map.

reference point – in the production of a map it can be the fixed *zero point* from which other positions are defined

reference system – a method of recording the position of places on a map so that they all relate logically to one another. Lines of *latitude* and *longitude* make up one reference system.

representative fraction – a mathematical method of indicating the *scale* of a map; 1/50,000 indicates that 1 unit on the map (a centimeter, for example) is equivalent to 50,000 units (50,000 centimeters, which equals 500 meters) on the ground

resection – a *surveying* method; at an unknown position the surveyor observes angles to known points to fix the new position

scale – the *ratio* of the size of a map to the area of the real world that it represents

sea level – the average level of the sea along the coastline; used as the *zero point* for measuring land heights, airplane *altitude*, and sea depths

surveying – the measuring of *altitudes*, angles, and distances on the land surface in order to obtain accurate positions of features that can be mapped. Hydrographic surveying of the oceans and seas also means measuring distances and angles between visible coastal positions, but the third dimension measured is depth rather than height.

symbol – a diagram, icon, letter, or character used on a map to represent a specific characteristic or feature

T-in-O maps – medieval European maps that show a very simplified outline of the three continents (only Europe, Africa, and Asia were known at the time) – the "T" shape. The "O" shape border represents an ocean surrounding Earth.

tacheometry – a *surveying* method; at a known position the surveyor observes bearing and distance to an unknown position to fix its location

telescope – a scientific instrument that uses lenses to make distance objects appear closer and larger

thematic map – a map that shows one particular aspect of the natural or human environment, such as transportation routes, weather patterns, tourism, population, vegetation, or geology

theodolite – a *surveying* instrument used to work out the angle between two observable points on Earth's surface viewed from a third point

topographic map – a map that shows natural features such as hills, rivers, and forests, and man-made features such as roads and buildings

total station – a *surveying* instrument used to measure both angle and distance at the same time on Earth's surface; the ideal instrument for *tacheometry*

triangulation – a *surveying* method that uses angles alone to work out the position of points on Earth's surface

trigonometry – math about angles and lengths in triangles, and mathematical formulas about them

tripod – a sturdy three-legged support on which *surveying* instruments are mounted

zero point or position – the point that defines the position of all other *reference points* on a map

Further Reading and Web Sites

Aczel, Amir D. *The Riddle of the Compass: The Invention That Changed the World*. New York: Harcourt, 2001.

Arnold, Caroline. *The Geography Book: Activities for Exploring, Mapping, and Enjoying Your World*. New York: Wiley, 2002.

Barber, Peter, and April Carlucci, eds. *The Lie of the Land*. London: British Library Publications, 2001.

Brown, Carron, ed. *The Best-Ever Book of Exploration*. New York: Kingfisher Books, 2002.

Davis, Graham. *Make Your Own Maps*. New York: Sterling, 2008.

Deboo, Ana. *Mapping the Seas and Skies*. Chicago: Heinemann-Raintree, 2007.

Dickinson, Rachel. *Tools of Navigation: A Kid's Guide to the History & Science of Finding Your Way*. White River Junction, VT: Nomad Press, 2005.

Doak, Robin S. *Christopher Columbus: Explorer of the New World*. Minneapolis, MN: Compass Point Books, 2005.

Ehrenberg, Ralph E. *Mapping the World: An Illustrated History of Cartography*. Washington, D.C.: National Geographic, 2005.

Field, Paula, ed. *The Kingfisher Student Atlas of North America*. Boston: Kingfisher, 2005.

Ganeri, Anita, and Andrea Mills. *Atlas of Exploration*. New York: DK Publishing, 2008.

Graham, Alma, ed. *Discovering Maps*. Maplewood, NJ: Hammond World Atlas Corporation, 2004.

Harvey, Miles. *The Island of Lost Maps: A True Story of Cartographic Crime*. New York: Random House, 2000.

Harwood, Jeremy. *To the Ends of the Earth: 100 Maps That Changed the World*. Newton Abbot, United Kingdom: David and Charles, 2006.

Haywood, John. *Atlas of World History*. New York: Barnes and Noble, 1997.

Hazen, Walter A. *Everyday Life: Exploration & Discovery*. Tuscon, AZ: Good Year Books, 2005.

Henzel, Cynthia Kennedy. *Mapping History*. Edina, MN: Abdo Publishing, 2008.

Jacobs, Frank. *Strange Maps: An Atlas of Cartographic Curiosities*. New York: Viking Studio, 2009.

Keay, John. *The Great Arc: The Dramatic Tale of How India Was Mapped and Everest Was Named*. New York: HarperCollins, 2000.

Levy, Janey. *Mapping America's Westward Expansion: Applying Geographic Tools And Interpreting Maps*. New York: Rosen Publishing, 2005.

Levy, Janey. *The Silk Road: Using a Map Scale to Measure Distances*. New York: PowerKids Press, 2005.

McDonnell, Mark D. *Maps on File*. New York: Facts on File, 2007.

McNeese, Tim. *Christopher Columbus and the Discovery of the Americas*. Philadelphia: Chelsea House, 2006.

Mitchell, Robert, and Donald Prickel. *Contemporary's Number Power: Graphs, Tables, Schedules, and Maps*. Lincolnwood, IL: Contemporary Books, 2000.

Oleksy, Walter G. *Mapping the Seas*. New York: Franklin Watts, 2003.

Oleksy, Walter G. *Mapping the Skies*. New York: Franklin Watts, 2003.

Resnick, Abraham. *Maps Tell Stories Too: Geographic Connections to American History*. Bloomington, IN: IUniverse, 2002.

Rirdan, Daniel. *Wide Ranging World Map*. Phoenix, AZ: Exploration, 2002.

Ross, Val. *The Road to There: Mapmakers and Their Stories*. Toronto, Canada: Tundra Books, 2009.

Rumsey, David, and Edith M. Punt. *Cartographica Extraordinaire: The Historical Map Transformed.* Redlands, CA: Esri Press, 2004.

Short, Charles Rennie. *The World through Maps.* Buffalo, NY: Firefly Books, 2003.

Smith, A. G. *Where Am I? The Story of Maps and Navigation.* Toronto, Canada: Fitzhenry and Whiteside, 2001.

Taylor, Barbara. *Looking at Maps.* North Mankato, MN: Franklin Watts, 2007.

Taylor, Barbara. *Maps and Mapping.* New York: Kingfisher, 2002.

Virga, Vincent. *Cartographia: Mapping Civilizations.* London: Little, Brown and Company, 2007.

Wilkinson, Philip. *The World of Exploration.* New York: Kingfisher, 2006.

Wilson, Patrick. *Navigation and Signalling.* Broomall, PA: Mason Crest Publishers, 2002.

Winchester, Simon. *The Map That Changed the World: William Smith and the Birth of Modern Geology.* New York: HarperCollins, 2001.

Zuravicky, Orli. *Map Math: Learning About Latitude and Longitude Using Coordinate Systems.* New York: PowerKids Press, 2005.

Online Resources

www.davidrumsey.com
The David Rumsey map collection. This online library contains around 20,000 historical and modern maps.

http://dma.jrc.it
The mapping collection of the European Commission Joint Research Center. Includes ineractive maps as well as maps documenting environmental and human disasters around the world.

http://etc.usf.edu/Maps/
The University of South Florida's online mapping library. The collection includes historical and modern maps from around the world.

www.lib.utexas.edu/maps
The University of Texas's online map library. The collection includes old CIA maps, historical maps, and thematic maps from around the world.

www2.lib.virginia.edu/exhibits/lewis_clark
An online exhibition at the University of Virginia with information on historic expeditions, including Lewis and Clark.

http://maps.google.com
Google's online mapping resource, includes conventional maps and satellite images for most of the world, as well as street-level photography of Western urban centers.

http://maps.nationalgeographic.com
National Geographic's online mapping service.

http://memory.loc.gov/ammem/gmdhtml/
Map collections from 1500–1999 at the Library of Congress. The collection includes maps made by early explorers, maps of military campaigns, and thematic maps on a variety of topics.

www.nationalatlas.gov
Online national atlas for the United States. Includes customizable topographic maps on a range of different themes.

http://strangemaps.wordpress.com
A frequently updated collection of unusual maps, from maps of imaginary lands to creative ways of displaying data in map form.

www.unc.edu/awmc/mapsforstudents.html
A large collection of free maps, covering many different subjects and regions, hosted by the University of North Carolina.

www.un.org/Depts/Cartographic/
  english/htmain.htm
United Nations mapping agency website. contains maps of the world from 1945 to the present day, including UN maps of conflict areas and disputed territories.

Index

Page numbers written in **boldface** refer to pictures or captions.

47

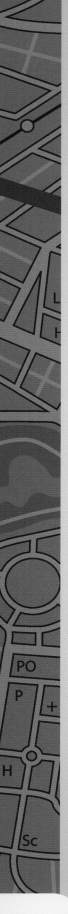